Cages
&
Other Places

Samuel Dees Wood

Cages
&
Other Places

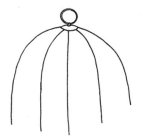

Poems By
Samuel Dees Wood

Illustrations By
C. Lary

WESTERN BOOK/JOURNAL PRESS
Printers & Publishers
RENO, NEVADA

ISBN: 0936029-55-2

Library of Congress Control Number: 00-132165

Manufactured in the United States of America

Western Book/Journal Press
Printers & Publishers
Reno, Nevada 89509

Library of Congress Cataloging-in-Publication Data
Wood, Samuel Dees, 1926-
Cages & Other Places
Poetry

To order additional copies of this book
Direct your order to:
P.O. BOX 7014
Reno, Nevada 89510

Dedicated

to

MABEL JULIAR NISBET

(who rekindled a dormant flame)

and to

GLORIA SPRINGER OBERG

(who nurtured it)

PREVIOUSLY PUBLISHED POEMS:

"LuLu" first appeared in *The Orient Express, Nov. 1985.* "Restoration (on a String)" appeared in *Prize Poems of the NFSPS, 1986.* "The Master Caller" and "Silhouettes" appeared in *Rime With a View* (Nevada Poetry Society, 1988). *"The Apple of Our Eye"* appeared in *The Best of 1992; Ohio Poetry Day Contest Awards.* "Yarn of the Norns" and "Autumn Lift" appeared in *Nevada Poets' Calendar, 1994.* "Pause" and "Something for Annabelle" appeared in *Nevada Poets' Calendar, 1995.* "A Lone Boot Strap" appeared in *Dance Notes,* Mar./Apr. 1997.

PREFACE

Having never fathered a book of poetry, I somehow feel obliged to explain its title. After I had written several dozen pieces, it occurred to me to wonder if there was a vein of common thought. It came as a surprise to discover that a number of poems were about being caged, if only metaphorically.

You may ask, "Do you see life as being caged?" Well, yes and no. There is blurring and ambiguity everywhere— not just in poetry. And, there is a freedom to understand both points of view— to see a transcendental purpose in the pattern. In short, to be inside and outside simultaneously.

Life is full of boundaries and parameters imposed by time, place, civilization, genes and upbringing. Recognizing multiplicity, I chose my title.

ACKNOWLEDGMENTS

Special appreciation to Lisa Corlee and Kathy Ouma who prepared a surprise desktop publication, *The Selected Poetical Works of Sam Wood*, on the occasion of my retirement in 1991.

Many thanks to other friends who also encouraged me by responding to my poems in constructive ways: Warren Bingham, Hilda Cao, Charmaine Donovan, Pj Doyle, Ann Gasser, Ardith Hayes, Maxine Jennings, Betsy Kennedy, Kathy Kerr, Keith Lucas, Jr., Barbara Stevens and Amy Zook.

And to my poetic family, members of the Nevada Poetry Society, I acknowledge that I couldn't have done this book without you. Craft matured through nourishment you provided.

Finally, my daughter Laura Wood has received a good many poems hot off my typewriter. She has commented on those she liked and kept a respectful silence for the others. She was the source for one of my favorite poems, "Once in Candelaria."

CONTENTS

CONTENTS

CONTENTS

PAUSE

a tiny opening
in my day
a tiny key will fit
when I turn it
I see you
do you
have a
key
for me

?

SOMETHING FOR ANNABELLE

Annabelle is pensive;
    Siren-songs from crocus
(Singing blue or yellow)
    Concentrate her focus.

Not-quite-in-love is not
    Enough, and daffodils
Are laughing at their joke:
    "No bee to press her frills!"

April quite suddenly
    Offers new flavoring:
Brawny but sensitive--
    Ready for savoring.

And he buzzes about
    Like a bee on a fling
While she smiles as she nods
    To her sisters of spring.

ONCE IN CANDELARIA*

"Just leave the work behind today,
   Just leave and walk the hills
Surrounding Candelaria;
   Forget the mines and mills."

From Harrigan's Saloon, just east,
   Came Belle, a dancehall girl,
To keep Ed Johnson's child the hours
   He let his day unfurl.

Then Johnson took his gun and dog,
   Took the road to Sodaville;
Star was barking as they veered
   To sagebrush up a hill.

Not far from town, a shadow moved
   Which only Star would see;
He sped away and then returned
   In some anxiety.

He circled Johnson, whined and gazed
   Toward town; "Forget it now,"
Said Johnson, "It's my day to walk;
   Forget your home and chow."

So they went a mile or more,
   And town was out of sight,
When, suddenly, Johnson knew
   That Star had taken flight.

He walked an hour more and thought
   His loyal dog would reappear,
Then turned and set his course for home
   And thought it mighty queer.

---

* Candelaria was a gold and silver mining town in Mineral County, Nev. It existed 1876-1939. This poem is a recasting and resetting of the sad tale of Gelert, a faithful dog for whom a village in Wales is named: Bedd Gelert (grave of Gelert)

Still, the day was more than tonic
  To a man who savors life,
Who has a son, who has a home
  And a soon-returning wife.

His house was empty when he reached it,
  With neither child nor Belle;
He called, then walked to the saloon,
  And he was mad as hell!

His spirit lightened as he saw
  His joyful Star come bounding
At seeing Johnson back in town—
  A grateful bay resounding.

In doing so, Star dropped a ball,
  A gift to Johnson's son;
From a bloody mouth it rolled,
  At Johnson's foot it spun.

He flinched in horror at the gore
  On Star, and panic was a flood;
Reason changed to terror, anger—
  His child was gone and here was blood!

A frenzied Johnson raised his rifle,
  Fired a bullet into Star;
The shot was followed by a sound:
  Infant laughter, not so far.

Rounding the saloon, he saw his boy
  Sitting by a mass of bloody fur;
A coyote met his match in Star
  Defending "Daddy's little cocklebur."

Then Belle came flouncing into view
  With her latest dancehall beau;
"Why'dja shoot yer dog?" she piped,
  And cast in stone the sad tableau.

"Desolation is a space that never fills;
  Guilt, a noose that never kills;
Forget the mines, forget the mills;
  Only leave and walk the hills."

TO RUTH

She moved with grace
And strength to lead— and strength to grow;
She moved with grace
And level gaze within the pace
Of deadlines and the need to know —
From dim to glimmer and to glow
She moved with grace.

MANY VARIOUS SINS

Singing from the radio:
                    "Jesus loves me,
                                but he cain't stand yew!"*

If King David had been gay,
        there would have been wives of convenience
        but when he walked at evening on his palace roof
        and saw a lovely woman (scheming) at her bath,
        she would have been only a flower in her garden.

He would not have lusted, not inquired
        not sent for this Bathsheba
        not lain with her, not begotten the son
        born to die for their transgression.

He would not have sent Uriah the Hittite into
        the thick of battle, married his widow, and
        brought the prophet Nathan down on him
        for robbing a poor warrior of his wife.

If King David had been gay,
        would he have been "a man after God's own heart"?
        Unlikely,
                        though he sinned in scarlet
                                and repented in gold.
"Jesus loves me,
                but he cain't stand yew!"

* A humorous song by the Austin (Tex.) Lounge Lizards.

NO REGRETS
(Musings of Don Giovanni)

September crickets fade to silence;
autumn chills their mating-burn.
They will cadence nights again;
my summer love cannot return.

    Take a ride to nowhere
    on the carousel of lust.
    Circle every perfect summer day;
    dismount, and all is dust.

    Winter sleep will settle agitation;
    loves are only seasons' wickets.
    I can see another summer;
    always, always, there are crickets.

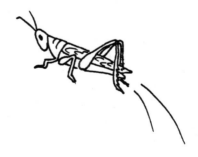

OF NOSES AND FACES

Her captive realm in 1943:
    children, husband, home and church.

She did well within the letter of maternal law
        but at night
       when color separated
   from the fragrance of her garden
     fireflies were substitutes
      with blinking questions
  — she yearned to finish college.

And she did —
      I saw her solving physics problems
          at the kitchen table
        when I was seventeen.

Mother's diploma was a waiting passport
    to somewhere, anywhere
    to a thinking world;
      what to do with it?

She felt a passive need for veto —
     waiting for a sign
  in those defensive times
  (when Daddy said, "Up,"
  and she said, "Down").

On the day she graduated, Daddy said
    (knowing nothing of reverse psychology),
    "Hon, why don't you get a teaching job?"

This was it ... and she replied (too quickly),
    "No, I think I'll stay
    right where I am."

And she did —
     like a little red hen —
          for
         more
         than
         fifty
         years.

THE VANITY OF TALL TREES

With heat of day diminishing, I found
sweet flesh, unbidden, standing at my door:
a youthful love, a later love which bound
her tryst of lavender to sycamore.

Not sought, but sent, a serendipity
in golden legs and arms with smile to set
a fragrance spreading through an older tree
to bring it into opulence — and yet ...

This tree has dreams of being tallest here.
If fate sends passion, let it surge for fame
to form my leaves and shape without a peer
and make me master in this garden game.

　To stand for love or fame, I have the growth
　to say: I will not choose; I want them both!

IN MY KEEPING
(an elegaic ode)

Lion dogs,
regal companions,
descendants of
living jewels
from Peking
palaces of
Empress Tzu Hsi
to England
and the world.

Oriental buds,
occidental flowers,
foliage in fur
unceasing,
pantaloons
sumptuous
and tails
cascading
softly over
formal coat
unchanging
at show
or play.

Lilliputian lion
fearless
tapered
royal carriage
patrician mien
at odds with
sailors'
rolling gait,
not hubris
but certainty
of power's
rightful place.

Level head
above
marmoset gaze,
side-framing
fringes
trying for
the floor;
flattened face
cat-nosed by
confrontation
with wall
of destiny
separating
archetypal
dogs;
massive head
holds
inscrutability
in darkly
hemispheric
knowing eyes,
luminosity
    in pools
    too deep
    to plumb
assessing with
tranquility
a loyal
biped master
and a world.

Hardly dogs,
aristocratic
lap-sized friends
prized by
older keeper
in more than
forty years
of relays,
most from
puppyhood
until their
sorrowed end.

Steady presence
in gravitas
or gaity
mirrors,
completes,
extends
the best
in me
by a few
pounds of
exquisite
existence,
my mantra
with a touch
for tie
with nature,
compass for
boundaries
of joy
or loss.

Most are
waiting on
a grassy bank
across
the river,

> She Loon
> Cho Cho
> Miss Chief
> Cameo
> Tu T'Sun
> Lu Lu
> Penny
> Kan Tu
> Tzu Tse
> Tu Tu
> Puffy
> Candy
> Red Legs

Patient
loving
Pekingese ...

MALE DUALITY

I

A man feels good
Anticipating love's delights;
A man feels good.
Inflating like a cobra's hood
When knowing that his lust incites,
And seeing self at lordly heights,
A man feels good!

II

This rose adored
Assures me I shall be its peer:
This rose adored.
Telepathy of sweetness toward
Its Adam breathes its meaning clear:
Perfection drapes the weakness near
This rose adored.

JANUARY 19

*(A birthday tribute to
a man long dead from
a man in black)*

I. At home

Perhaps I will not go this year, for cold
and pain discourage two midwinter drives
   past midnight through a sleeping Baltimore.

But six white roses challenge early dawn,
along with cognac to be drunk for warmth
   (and empathy with Edgar Allan Poe)

Two cemeteries wide apart demand
my long and self-imposed imperative
   be satisfied this date in every year.

So now my pilgrimage begins to her:
my Annabelle who died in '48,
   immortal now to me because of Poe.

The love of mine was like the love of his:
denied by circumstance of "chilling wind"
   to end in separation incomplete.

For she is with me now forever through
the power of Poe's verses as he wills
   a part of me to be a youth again.

II. With Annabelle

And so, past midnight, standing by your stone
the past becomes his Annabel in you
   and you are mine in empathy with him.

I lay three roses on your grave and sip
the cognac's warmth as clouds unveil the moon
   and seem to form a haloed cameo.

And I remember, on a summer night
you read remembrance of his Annabel
in verses binding me to you to her.

And with your passing, Poe became the bond
which held my soul to yours, and I devoured
his works, digesting anguish turned to use.

He died in 1849 and dropped
the bitter cup which I lift up to drink:
transcendence in a cup of sympathy.

Goodbye, sweet Annabelle, I leave again
to be with Poe at his Westminster plot,
to touch the braid of you and me and him.

III. With Poe

And now at 3:00 A.M. I kneel beside
your grave this forty-third (and hardest) year
of all my visits — paying my respects.

I drink to you: the craft, the genius in
a soul that plumbed the desolation loosed
within us all when terror strips us bare.

Oh, Master Raven, I am haunted by
your "Nevermore" which touches all of life
and breeds a melancholy clung to loss.

Your Annabel — my Annabelle — are one
and we are one, but I had time to heal —
to find a kindred voice to speak my thoughts.

In chill of early dawn I drink again
and pledge another tribute in a year;
remember, I am almost twice your age.

And now I lay three roses on your grave
beside the bottle which I share with you
in drinking to a wisp of memory.

TO ANNETTA
(whose bosom it was)

Late evening at a sleepy laundromat
A pleasant, older woman measures soap
As Old Whiskers nurses a fuzzy hope
Caught in senility's lariat.

He touches her plump arm and has his say;
He asks if he can touch her pretty breast.
"No, you can't!" (as though caught undressed)
"Get away,
           just get away!"

Old duffers slink away when told —
Dismissed as bits of trivia or trash
Which dim like afterglow of photoflash
If not stored in subconscious afterhold.

The woman's cancer and her surgeon meet;
Mastectomy's assault leaves something sought;
Anesthesia's prompting speaks her thought:
"Save it,
         send it to Old Whiskers down the street."

IN A SPANISH GALLEY (1588)

Stretch, summer evening ... sweetest languor
    Lies along exhausted arms forsaken
To these hellish oars on rosy water.
    Neither body nor my soul yet taken ...

"Row, you English dogs, or feel
    The lash across your scrawny backs!
Row, or soon the Virgin Bitch
    Will feed you to her Channel packs!"

Aye! Queen Bess shall smite these bastards!
    Sir Francis is her strong right arm;
Her hand shall pluck the Spanish duck —
    Our ships and homes shall come to no great harm.

So stalk us! catch us! pound us! sink us!
    Slaves on board can stand the pain.
Better die by wounds or drowning
    Than to row the victors back to Spain!

THE NEW SANTA CLAUS

I

All knew how very tired he was
    When Santa blessed his bailiwick;
None understood the time had come
    To choose a new St. Nick.

"My dears," he whispered, "any one
    Of you can fill my shoes because ...
Every elf with nurturing
    Can become a Santa Claus."

"A secret long ago was passed
    To me; I pass it on to you;
Each of you must read this scroll
    For it explains what you must do."

"One of you next Christmas Eve
    Will sweep into the sky
With the planet's wealth of giving;
    Time will prove your inner eye."

When Santa died in early spring,
    In the Hall of Gingerbread,
Not one elf could tell the year
    When first he wore the suit of red.

II

Lively, loyal little workers,
    The elves moved quickly past their grief
(As suggested in the scroll);
    They knew election would be brief.

The chosen elf was loved by all:
    A tiny slice of Christmas spice;
The reindeer stamped their hooves to cheer
    As Hardy grinned and spun 'round twice.

The cup of giving having passed,
    Days were filled with ho, ho, ho-ing,
Eating as the scroll required,
    Height and wisdom growing, growing.

Hardy's stature as December came
    Was all the happy elves had hoped;
Gifts and Santa almost ready,
    They puffed with pride in having coped.

This year, renewal takes the reins
    When Santa leaps into his sleigh;
The how and where and who are planned —
    Your understanding your bouquet!

THREE PERFECTED LADIES

This love I feel is triple dip
   by inward flip
   into three pools
   where passion rules.
Unbridled wavelets radiate
   and sublimate
   the flaw of one
   to flaw of none
as each perfects the others' charms,
   extending arms
   of love to me
   with certainty ...

THOUGHTS OF THE PRESIDENT
(Sept. 11, 1998)

Fall is coming;
   will I join the flaming
   brotherhood of leaves
   this year?

The Starr is out,
   winds are blowing
   through the House and Senate
   with mighty gusts from puffers
   like that old windbag Moynihan.

Hounds of Congress are baying
   beneath their harvest moon
   as they set about treeing
   Brer Possum from Arkansas.

Whatever happens,
   I was
   by the grace of God
   twice President
   of these United States.

But,
   the sexual revolution
   flowered in the White House.

Roman emperors knew it well:
   lust is a spring
   atop the legs of power.

I brought myself to this
   swing of the pendulum —
   not equating penitence
   with resignation.

Did King David abdicate
   when the prophet Nathan
   delivered a rebuke from God?

Yet his remorse so stirred Jehovah
   that David came to be proclaimed
   a man after God's own heart.

Scarlet sins are natural sins,
   yoked, perhaps, to strength
   within a man or woman —
   the vigor of wrong
   may feed the right of the other.

Noblesse oblige is my contrition;
   let those with lesser sins
   be allowed to cast their stones ...

WE CALLED HIM OLD MAN FAT MAN

What is sown is perishable,
What is raised is imperishable.
I Cor. 15:42b (R.S.V.)

Eden's descendants displaying their glow:
    Peaches voluptuous, glory full-blown;
Looming are seed from the fruit of this hour;
    After the peach the stone ...

        He strides with purpose
           along the sidewalk
           moving north
           (never south)
           toward downtown
           flourishing his cane
           with every-other step.

        Old Man Fat Man has the
           jaunty grace of a boulevardier
           somewhat *déclassé* in
           khaki pants, red galluses,
           straw hat and full shirt
           buttoned at the neck
           in heat of 90°.

        He has the air of knowing
           a secret and of going
           "there" to take care
           of urgent business.
           Though not suave enough
           to be a spy, he seems
           certain to reach a
           mysterious destination
           not too far because
           he walks every day
           and (terribly important)
           we never see him return.

Old Man Fat Man
   is a walk-on
   to mark a moment
   in our sleepy drama,
   his motivation quite unknown
   (and what can be his name?)
   Yet the cycle of his
   walk ceases unnoticed.
   We know it only when,
   one day, some kid says,
   "Has anyone seen him lately?"

He is gone with the 1930s,
   summer in Oklahoma,
   cicadas singing in the elms,
   roller skating where he walked,
   'Monopoly' on the front porch,
   rubbergun wars, stilts,
   games with fireflies.
   No one misses Old Man Fat Man
   but he has not gone unnoticed.

A DROP OF FIERY RAIN

This craving for remembrance is in vain;
For afterglow of ego dispossessed
Bowls yearn to catch a drop of fiery rain.

Their souls are branded with the mark of Cain,
But they, in wan despair, are frightened lest
This craving for remembrance is in vain.

Their strength subdued by cracks and age and strain
(And bold design become a blur), the best
Bowls yearn to catch a drop of fiery rain.

They try with clutching wisdom to retain
A spark beyond their use, but in their test
This craving for remembrance is in vain.

To yield themselves with grace when life is bane,
But will to hold an image sweetly dressed,
Bowls yearn to catch a drop of fiery rain.

And so, at last, the signal; and their train
Moves through the night along the tracks of rest;
This craving for remembrance is in vain,
Bowls yearn to catch a drop of fiery rain!

DOTS WITHOUT END, AMEN

Seething
during luncheon —
begrudging food he turned
into his ugly self — I wished
him dead.

Reason
whispered deftly
that dot is dot at my
vast predestined pointillistic
table.

RESOLUTIONS KEPT

Four warts on my existence had to go!
Consensus thought removal would be slow;
Loose language was the sin to blaze the way:
Hell froze over at one o'clock today.

A deficit of niceness must be quit —
My tongue be harnessed list'ning to a twit;
Ah, kindness! — now I'm really making hay:
Hell froze over at two o'clock today.

When age conspires a drift to lotusland,
I must jump ship or find myself ill-manned;
Inertia moderated is the play:
Hell froze over at three o'clock today.

"Half-empty" is a feeling hard to quell;
Dark thoughts half-fill my cup and yet I'm well;
A different vessel— ah! ... for Beaujolais!
Hell froze over at four o'clock today.

With all your weaknesses in tow,
You give a break to those Below;
Your friends will marvel at the spell—
And, what is more, you'll shake up Hell!

PAST MIDNIGHT IN THE HALL

Five are quartered in my house
  — there is never only one.
I sense they wait impatiently by day
  — desperation in the walls —
where emptiness looks out on
fullness in the game of living.

I cannot hide from them:
  remnants of half-thoughts,
  half-fears — remainders of childhood.

They seldom appear; but when they do,
  it is sudden, unexpected,
  like a fall through a trap-door
  in hall or other place of transition
  between here and there
  when psychic gears are being shifted,
  when the clap of orange light or
  zap of blue current cuts the darkness.

Five orange ovals float about,
  some large — all teasing —
  tempting a human moth hypnotically
  to bluff, despite a paralyzing dread.

If, in a moment of sentient courage,
  I touch a floater,
  I feel at rest, feel at peace
  in touching light beyond light.

For I think, "They are here for a reason;
          I am being told to make
          things right, for there is
          so very little time."

Without telepathy, I know; and knowing,
  wonder what my course should be.

So I walk, stalking a tantalizing light;
  but focus premeditates its disappearance:
  lengthening downward and sinking into the
  floor, followed by companions one by one.

My moment of bravery is past;
  I switch dimensions of space and
  they are held behind a wave of light.

Ecstasy of fear has deflowered tonight
  and become bread and butter for tomorrow.

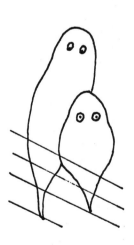

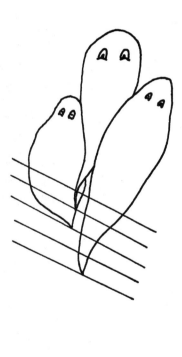

VALEDICTORY

Chancellor Bismarck said it:
SIXTY-FIVE IS THE AGE TO RETIRE
(Let's hear it for the chancellor!)

Retirement is *terra incognita.*

I must feel my way through it,
decide how to occupy it
(if, indeed, it can be occupied
when its magnetic boundary is
that unshaped but finite mystery)

But this is the time to disdain markers

a time for turning out — or in (or both)
for gearing up — or winding down (or both)

You see the problem ...

Candide said it:
WE MUST CULTIVATE OUR GARDEN
(Let's hear it for Candide!)

NEVADA ONCE

They shaped a place
Where body and the spirit tanned;
They shaped a place
Where sage surrendered iron lace
To flowers on the barren land
Where space encircled their demand
They shaped a place.

SINCERELY YOURS, BILL

Why can't I keep from reaching out
to tawdry flowers far outclassed?
"No touch, no pluck!" the hissing shout
of Hillary in bedtime blast.

Assuming I am not miscast,
why can't I keep from reaching out?
I sail without a phallic mast,
my compass is no roustabout.

Yet I am deemed a brilliant lout
by old and newer friends aghast.
Why can't I keep from reaching out
to flowers soft and hourglassed?

I see a harbor at the last —
perhaps I'm old, perhaps I'm stout.
Until that time when now is past
why can't I keep from reaching out?

LAMENT OF A COLOSSUS

Hard to believe:
   almost 500 years since
   I was set before
   admiring Florence
   in a plaza for
   the universe to marvel.

Still standing in
   thoughtful concentration
   with my sling prepared —
   no defense against
   voyeurs of the world —
   clothed only in white marble,
   head and heart and loins
   petrified.

David, unarrayed,
   a Jewish lad uncircumcised
   by a master of cutting tools —
   manhood diminished by
   constraint of art.

Is this *lèse majesté*
   to a lover of many concubines,
   to a husband of many wives,
   to the father of Solomon,
   to a king of Israel?

Yes, a monarch on display,
   stripped to an ideal of
   youth by Michelangelo.

Still, strange irony:
   greater glory in this form
   than when my form was flesh.

Which the masterpiece:
   prototype of me,
   or stone of me?

Smells of humanity
    gather in this museum;
    wine, perfume,
    garlic, lust
    mingle and rise with
    awe of humanity
    in a focused, still,
    erotic, bursting moment.

Slaying Goliath was nothing
    compared to ogling
    by twittering women and
    the empathic embarrassment
    of men gazing up
    with thoughtful eyes.

A fig leaf would be nice, or
    better still, a pair of jeans ...

SILHOUETTES

Hills are moving through the night —
   their tops and valleys dip and rise
   in moonlight blending all into a hum
   of love between the earth and skies.

These are not the shoulders
     backs
          and breasts of youth.

Arms and legs are old
     but intertwine
           in timeless worship
           in the lay of life:
Silver passion magnified by size.

DELILAH REMEMBERS

Not the best that I had
for he loved like a child
in a mixture of show
and delight in my hair.

He was mine in cascade
of his lust in my glow
and the moonbeams and myrrh
of a Philistine trap.

Not a slave to his touch,
yet his strength was a brooch
to be flaunted, displayed
as adorning my flesh.

I grew tired of him soon,
my strong Samson in love,
for I dreaded excess
of his vigor in joy.

In the flicker of thought
that betrayal could come,
he loved flirting with fate
and its lure of deceit.

"Oh, Samson,
why do you tease?"

My rebukes for his tricks
wore down stubborn conceit
when dissembling wore thin
and he crumpled to truth.

All the silver aside,
it was time he was gone —
no remorse and no pain
at the end of my game.

When the light in his eyes
became night, and his rank
was reduced to a slave,
I was richer and free.

When the temple came down
by return of his strength,
I was sporting with more
but was happy with less.

As his memory fades
to a saintly pastel,
he can whisper soft taunts
as I lie with another.

"Oh, Samson,
can't you just sleep?"

PUTTING THINGS AWAY

night was vacillating

        skies were clear
          then cloudy
        and clear again
            though set to storm
              with maybe rain to fall

night was vacillating

        thoughts were clear
          then vague
        and clear again
            suppressing weary tears
            too tired to fall

decisive scissors

            snipped the past

    (or so it seemed)

                    and whispers from old loves
                        were laid in velvet

                (or so it seemed)

LULU

You explode into the room, toenails clicking
like castanets across the kitchen floor.

Pint-size lion from Peking,
I have no fin of shark or curlew's liver
or breast of quail for you today.

But I have here a fortune cookie —
not your usual canine fare,
but a Chinese luncheon souvenir —
which I give you out of curiousity.

You hesitate, then take with cautious mood
this unknown food; now, with decision,
crunch its low-sweet blandness.

Because the cookie now is part of you,
the message fallen from it is yours too.

I lift the slip — as you look up —
and read aloud your fortune:
YOUR HEART IS PURE, YOUR MIND IS CLEAR,
AND YOU ARE DEVOUT.

I whoop with laughter as I sweep you up before me;
you sneeze with pleasure
and a cool mist sprays my face.

I laugh again, in mock dismay, and look into your
large and dark and luminous eyes of love.

And I say, "LuLu, you are into leather,"
as I lightly tap the black lunette between your
eyes.

I move to put you down, but your fur delights my
fingers, and your twelve-pound superwarmth stays
my hands.

I draw you to me and caress your silken fringes,
and a scent (secure, maternal, timeless)
stirs some lost remembrance.

But only for a moment. From the hall, intrusive
chimes remind discreetly that one can never
linger.

TO ANY FAUST

You please
dark Mephistopheles
when evil is your pilot light
for appetite,
igniting all your lust
from flash to gust.
And, all content,
your pilot vents consent
for darkest bliss;
flickers and shadows writhe from this
dark Mephistopheles
you please.

THE ROSE THAT GOT AWAY

I

YESTERDAY : THE DANCE

Crescendo,

> twisting hips and torso
> tease her into face to face
> after I lead her turning
> to dip and rise on slippers

> > of glossy pearl
> > barely touching
> > this burnished
> > rosewood floor.

In a male hand, she is a rose,

> > a fragrance without a thorn.

> We are floating
> scarcely rowing

> > on a lavender sea of silk
> > over waves of geometry in
> > rosy squares of parquetry.

Steady pressure of her hand

> > guides the tiller of Eros
> > who lightens the foot and the eye
> > under cascading glitter of chandeliers
> > in a room of gold and pink and cream
> > in a hall of shadow and glow.

The dance ends, alas,

> > and I find that there IS a thorn
> > (she calls it a "fiancé")

TODAY : THE GARDEN

This twisting path

        guides me on a summer day
        through the stalwart
        honesty of hollyhocks

                to rows of mercurial roses:

        tidy precision circumscribing
        them: a rectangle bordered by
        tiny guard of creeping phlox.

I marvel at my handiwork

          as He who walked another garden and knew
            first the sweet fragrance of a rose.

My hand has set each bush into its square of earth
      — soil and seasons have been my servants
for the velvet harvest stretching out before me.

Warm sunlight lies gently on my arm as I reach out
              in languor
                to savor
           through my fingers
            a love reflected
         from a master bush:

                  an archetypal rose.

A bud arouses an appetite for opening —
      whets an urge for petals of flesh
which did not open in gardens past.

I pause at "Queen Elizabeth," a gentle pink
        and think of other queens —
           some in ballrooms —
              some elsewhere.

I feel a tug of love at "Tropicana"
share its red orange breath
and feel a red orange glow.

Reds flaunt, in demanding shapes and shades,
the very blood of love

expanding,
lifting
islands of renewal

so wide,
so elastic
in nights of
youthful flush.

Finally, before a special bush:
keepsake of a breath of fantasy so long ago,
this lavender reminder of a soft and fragrant
evening when what might have been was not...

III

TIMELESS : THE DREAM

Rosewood everywhere — flowers skittering
from the woodwork
scourged by a hollyhock.

Three roses glide across a diamond floor
three graces hand in hand
pink grace
yellow grace
red grace.

"Thorns, we need thorns," they cry.

Three handsome thorns appear, "Mozart sent us!:"

Fantastic: being in Mozart's head!
I, I, I, watching through his eyes.

"Assume the position, assume the position at once," he orders.

Each thorn offers an arm
each thorn makes a leg
each rose curtseys and accepts.

"First a minuet," announces Mozart.

Dancing —
and I am out of Mozart's head
moving toward the line.

"Stop," he cries, "you are a thorn without a rose
get a rose at once!"

I am running, flying, falling.
Where is the garden? Where is my rose?

"Any rose will do," Mozart thunders, "even a wild one!"

No! I must have a cultured one.
Is there a lavender one somewhere?
Perhaps in the prisms of the chandelier?

I rise to the occasion
for I am a thorny, thorny, thorn.

A moon comes up blue— my lavender rose could be only a pink.
She tries to hide in her skirt of green
as I pick a leaf to show my strength;
she braces to be picked.

Mozart shouts, "Couples ready,

a gigue — assume the position!"

The three graces and their thorns

dance around us
and away

as we hop
and turn
and twist.

She is more lavender
than they are

pink and red and yellow.

She says, "You are the thorn
I have always waited for,"
and sings, "Yes, I am your

partner now,
I am,
I am."

Mozart groans, "Not mine, not mine — MY music or you
will never,
never merge."

Lightning thunders

the graces and my rose run
screaming into the woodwork
and I am left with the other thorns.

Lazy Susan, turning, brings the Queen of the Night,

"Mozart created me —

I can separate you for all time,
all time;
all roses will be thornless
to the four corners of
endless squares of parquetry."

Brilliance from Mozart's face dazzles her away.

"Roses, return to your thorns — assume the position!"

A pavane,

four couples weaving in and out
of columns to
a yawning arch
with blossoms
pendant.

"Red and pink and yellow trinity,
heap diamonds on the head of
this lavender rose and declare to her,

'This is your wedding day.'"

Mozart is waiting in the bower,
sunlight on his head and hand.

Lavender glows to white and she says,

"I do — probably."

Clash of cymbals!

Mozart demands,

"Now, Queen of the
Night,
what do you say?"

A black rose rises from the floor to snicker,

"Dub her the fourth
grace;
dub her,
dub her,

do!"

Mozart giggles and commands,
"Assume the position,
roses and thorns,
assume the position."

IN AN HOUR OF NEED

Her Thoughts

Into night with the fireflies and tightening desire
  (after music and party, the dance and his plan)
  with an ache from the will of my flesh to the flash
  of submission when I will envelope this man.
But the flush of the apple (though red — oh, so red)
  will diminish by reason when I have been fed.

But I go — I must go
  for he circles my waist
    as he leans to his prize
      and he leads where he wills.

His Thoughts

She is ready for taking, and I am her man.
  All the dancing, the sweet-talk and pressure have paid
  for past pleasure (about to repeat) as we move
  to the deep-grassy knoll in the woods for a raid.
Oh, the weapon is ready, the target is sure
  when a woman is willing and hardly demure.

And the shame that she feels
  will be gone when she lies
    with a man on the make
      and she gives as he takes

Thoughts of God

They are made in my image, but they are not gods
  and they rush to their coupling, abusing the fire
  of a woman, the fire of a man to burn clean
  on a night for renewal of strength through desire.
I will open their eyes with the touch of my hand
  and burn lust into love from the flame I have fanned.

Then their need shall be bound
  by the ribbon of love
    which unwinds from a spool
      in the colors of light.

48

WOOL GATHERING

When sheep surround me as I rest,
Late summer whispers *laissez-faire*;
All boundaries are flower-blessed.

A book is laid beside me lest
It fall from fingers unaware
When sheep surround me as I rest.

Kind fences square the garden's quest;
Wild tangles, hedges, vistas swear
All boundaries are flower-blessed.

This patio is doubly best
With dogs and finches here and there
When sheep surround me as I rest.

Warm scents of afternoon attest
The seeds of spring which now declare
All boundaries are flower-blessed.

My soul and garden are abreast;
Beloved corral is everywhere
When sheep surround me as I rest;
All boundaries are flower-blessed.

THE BIRTHDAY CLOCK

I

He was surprised when we brought it: a
Stately, mahogany, grandfather clock
Straight as a soldier to guard all the
Hours of an octogenarian cock.

Grandfather stared at the gift in a
Mesmerized way as we touted its size,
Bragging how lucky Felicia and
I had become in our search for a prize.

Seemingly hoping the powerful
Timepiece was only some very tall fun
(Viewing the clock as competitor)
Grandfather doubtfully asked, "Does it run?"

"Let there be sound!" laughed Felicia in
Starting the clock, and the pendulum swung,
Catching the light in its brass as a
Sepulchral rhythm attached to its tongue.

Speaking in nuance to each of us,
Ticking hypnotically, timelessly sure —
Measuring bits of existence seemed
Restful and peaceful and endlessly pure.

Cousin Felicia looked pleased with the
Mood, but I noticed that he looked confused.
"Ticks like the beat of the heart of an
Ol' banty rooster," our grandfather mused.

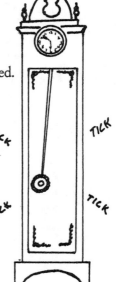

Then he added, "But what if it stops?"
"Oh, you just set it and wind it," I said.
Grandfather paused as if something were
Lacking — I felt a sensation of dread.

Cake and champagne and a gossip with
Grandfather ended the intimate fête;
Gaity reigned and the ticking was
Quietly ruffling no feathers as yet.

50

I returned home with a satisfied
Smile and the thought the gift seemed so right:
Quality, harmony, dignity
Merged man and the clock — merged shortness with height.

Similar thoughts were occurring to
Grandfather, I was to learn very soon,
Though my equations were mightily
Wrong for he marched to a different tune.

Calling late Saturday night, he was
Testy because, as he said, "I can't sleep —
It's the synchronicity of the
Beast — not so loud — just a persistent creep."

" Is it the clock?" I asked Grandfather.
"Beautiful piece, but the beat of it still
Bothers me terribly ... seem to be
Trapped by its rhythm and bent to its will."

"You'll get used to it — takes a few
Days of adjustment — It's just a new sound;
It's only doing its work so that
You can forget it each time when it's wound."

"But if it should stop before I wake ... "
Grandfather paused, and I carefully said,
"Certainly nothing so slight — not the
Stopping of ticking while you are in bed."

"You understand," he admitted. "A
Clock is a clock and a heart is a heart;
Letting this voodoo undo me is
Moving the target for meeting a dart."

"Right! Absolutely correct in your
Thinking," I said, though I wondered a bit
Whether his burst of resolve was a
Wistful assurance unmasked by his wit.

Grandfather died in his sleep on the
Following Monday — discovered by Lee
Coming at eight for a morning of
Cleaning and banter enlivened by tea.

When I arrived and she opened the
Door of the tiny apartment, I walked
Into the arms and the grief of a
Woman who cared, and we mourned as we talked.

Grandfather peacefully lay as if
Thirty-nine of his forty winks were done.
"Naps are practice for that final sleep,"
Once he said, "the flesh has 'lost and won.'"

Silence lay over the rooms as we
Paused, being lost in our memories' mix;
It was then that two thoughts connected:
The clock ... I looked ... it had stopped at six.

"Which six?" I wondered, for Grandfather's
Shoulders were warm — which suggested his time
Might have come during, or after, he
Recently roused to the sound of a chime.

Hale to the end, he had lived a good
Life, but the clock was a shadow which lay
Over these dismal two weeks when what
Seemed a magnificent toy had its way.

Cousin Felicia was never to
Know that our gift was an ill-fitting coat,
Though in a letter received on the
Day of his funeral, Grandfather wrote:

"Dearest Felicia,
    It's Sunday and
Raining in Kansas! The clock has just stopped.
Silence! ... it's golden (with diamonds
Strewn in a kitchen that needs to be mopped)"

YARN OF THE NORNS

Waiting ... something good will happen;
   flowers fly in wishful thinking
      (fathered by hope, mothered by need)
        die from truth's relentless linking.

Waiting ... something bad will happen;
   brambles, thorns and kindred fellows
      stalk, but run amok — entangling
        in the fuzz of pinks and yellows.

THE OPEN MAN

The way it is, my love, is this: I am
The whisper of despair tonight — as though
Some message did not come today — a toll
Unpaid has left me open and alone.

    Clothe me ... no, unclothe me.
      The price of cover is too dear;
   I long to bare my soul,
      But bolts of cloth are everywhere.

The day, beloved, was full — but empty too.
I moved my hand and all imaginings
And possibilities converged to bring
The afternoon into a total gain.
But as I turned to leave my battlefield
Of ego, talent, intellect and drive,
It seemed not I — but anyone at all —
Had won and lost; the day was but a sham.

    Complete me, dearest one ...
      These arcs of resolution serve
   To bind the moon to us
      As straightest rays caress this curve.

By dazzling day your bedded god creates
A vast and complicated uselessness;
The blot and blur of night will signify
Contrition and return to formlessness.
But face tomorrow's tired successes I
Cannot — unless, my love, you armor me
With skin too thick to pierce, a victor's rod
And fig-leaf as a bulwark and a shield.

Clothe me ... no, unclothe me.
   The price of cover is too dear;
I long to bare my soul,
   And you have seen it lying here.

The altar of this night is now the space
Where emptiness and consolation lace
Our matching hunger — so that flesh has ceased
To faint ... and hunger shared becomes a feast!

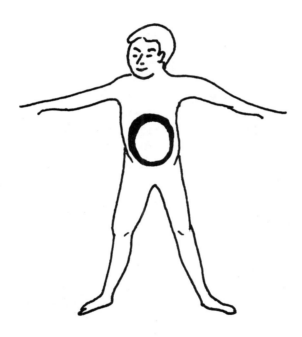

DELIVERED TO HISTORY

November broods and backward looks at times
Which it has passed, the fairer and the harsh.
Again denuded, trees and rawest points
Of failures, burdens, losses lie exposed
As baggage of the year.
                Eleventh month!
It came so quickly, yet we know our feet
Are foreordained to walk a flowered path
Beset by slight successes, mild defeats
Or worse ... converging with advancing grey.
Ahead, December's denouement; her spool
Unwinds the season's red and green and gold,
To mend with color weariness and wear.
This year shall be delivered; pangs of birth
Assure that best and worst are times of worth.

CATHARSIS ON THURSDAY AFTERNOON

"O blast! O damn! O hell! O shut
the door — just let me be
alone to float at sea
or I will likely bust a gut!"
And then the phone, a call
so urgent but so small,
an earnest need from Lilliput.

AT HOME WITH FUR AND FEATHERS

They speak to share their thoughts among themselves
   on Christmas Eve: this animal, that bird,
   in cages near the tinselled ambience
   of glitter and glow of sumptuous fir.

White guinea pig among the birds:
   simple, pink-eyed Popcorn chews his
   hay — neighbor to winged elegance —
   and speaks, "How pretty all this is!"

Red, splendid parrot says, "Heh, heh;
   is this your wisdom that you say?
   How clever is bucolic wit
   from one who nibbles prairie hay!"

Comes little sigh, "How pretty all this is."

The whydah, elegant, long-tailed,
   vain, looks down and laughs a riddle:
   "Tell me why, Rump-Without-A-Tail,
   some have so much, some so little?"

Popcorn repeats, "How pretty all this is!"

      Then, from many tiny heads
      comes babbling bird discourse.
       Says the combasou,
         "I don't have to be kind
          because I am so strong!"
       Says the Gouldian finch,
         "I don't have to be useful,
          because I am so beautiful."
       Says the tiny zebra finch,
         "I don't have to be smart
          because I am petite."
       Says the lovebird,
         "We shut out the world
          because we are a pair."

Popcorn again, "How pretty all this is!"

And then he squeals and nestles for the night
when lights go out (except the glowing tree)
while colored shadows dance across the walls
as feathers ruffle for the peace of sleep ...

with birds' last thought, "How pretty all this is ... "

THE OTHER TREE

The antidote to God's tremendous will,
   it stood unflaunting, modest and unused,
      it's fruit more potent than the doom which fused
         man's taint into eternal codicil.
This leafy witness to the tempter's skill
   perceived two likenesses of God abused,
      heard helpless, aproned, primal flesh accused,
         and grieved that seized morality could kill.

Ideas live, though men and leaves decay.
   So God redreamed his dream and with his breath
      revived the tree as flesh (through love) to say,
"Millennia proclaim your night is rife
   with longing to escape from bond with death;
      now Mother Mary is the Tree of Life."

OUT OF ITS CAGE

"I will tread them in mine anger, and will trample them in my fury ... "
(Isaiah 63:3) — Quoted by Jonathan Edwards (1703-1758) in his sermon
"Sinners in the Hands of an Angry God."

I am not fond of this one   but he needs exercise
    and is gentle enough as I lift this puff of squirming
    softness from the cage and place him in a plastic
    orb and secure the hatch.

Rolling around the kitchen   careening in enjoyment
    as he strokes his curving room   rolling, rolling
    as his legs propel him rudderless here and there
    against chair-and-table legs and massive juttings.

I leave him to his captive pleasure in an errant car
    and savor magnanimity bestowed on this lesser being
    sharing recreation as I sit and watch TV.

Twenty minutes pass   diminished sound jerks me to
    awareness of the silence from the kitchen
    the rolls and bumps have stopped and the organizer
    of this enterprise rushes to investigate.

I see an empty orb   see its hatch four feet away
    and know I have a hamster on the loose.

Terms of thought are battle strategy: closing every
    door for limiting his field   lights ablaze in
    every room   flashlight supplementing
    search behind curtains, furniture and any
    micro-place a tiny fugitive might hide.

I feel a nagging panic   for the order of things
    is topsy-turvy   the rodent has upset the
    natural balance and become master of
    his destiny within my space.

Room-by-room inspection tells me that he has
    eluded me for now   but I believe escape
    has led him to a back-bedroom.

With the house compartmentalized, I turn
to minor household tasks and give him time to move —
searching rooms from time to time.

A half-hour later, I open the bedroom door and
see a scrap of russet frantic to squeeze behind a
cabinet   I reach down to grasp him, but he slips
forward, resisting rightful return to his cage
I grab again and have him in my hand.

As I lift him from the floor he flexes with
unexpected strength   I tighten my grip
he bites (in frustration)   I tighten (in anger)
he bites again.

(Kill it   kill it   kill it!)

With murder in my heart and power in my hand
I hurl this ungrateful creature against
the closet door   he falls and hits the carpet running
I am past reason   I stomp him once
I stomp him twice   but still he runs
I put my foot on him   he cannot move.

I glove myself with a garment handy   seize and
return him to his cage   he creeps unrepentent
to a corner and turns to stare defiantly.

While looking at a bloody thumb and garment
I realize   a hundred-fifty pounds have
triumphed over a few ounces of flesh and fur;
fury is recaged as reason broods.

The coin of anger has flipped and spun
coming up remorse for unbridled wrath
for failure to secure him in a way
consistent with *noblesse oblige*.

How terrible to be an angry god!

NOTES OF FEELING

"What am I to you?" he pleaded —
Cutting through advice he needed.
"Friend ... a friend," I countered quickly,
But the word came through as sickly —
   Too glib, too pat, too thin!
Anguish strummed a chord of healing
Formed from notes of honest feeling;
Filtered harshness, accusation,
Served a more than token ration —
   To feed, to soothe, to win ...

WASHDAY IN 1920

At rooster crow of summer dawn
Ida braids her heavy hair,
accepting washday with a yawn
at her lyesoap path of care.

How soon the married country belle
performs domestic rub-a-dubs
in raising rivers from the well
for boiling-pot and rinsing-tubs.

Water drawn, she coaxes working flames
beneath the pot and leaves it heating.
In her kitchen she revives and tames
the cast iron stove for morning eating.

Twelve are fed and dishes done,
seven hurry their escape to school,
two are left to see the wash begun
as a torrid day unwinds its spool.

Poke bonnet, Ida's antidote
to lash of blazing sun,
eyes in refuge from its steady gloat —
Yetta would not be seen in one.

Coquette of the increasing brood,
she dawdles while remembering a touch
as Ida stirs with placid certitude:
every task is just an hour or such.

Washboards, soap and endless heat
as clothes are lifted from the boiling pot;
cool water in the final rinse is sweet,
cranking wringers crush the washday plot.

Ida in her rocker in the shade
hums and gives herself to dozing;
rest is good ... supper to be made ...
another washday closing, closing ...

On her lap the bonnet lies;
she thinks of how it shapes her soul;
heat of life has made bread rise,
mixing it has been her role.

Nothing done with any shoddiness;
she can say with perfect sense,
"Cleanliness is next to Godliness,"
While standing by the cowlot fence.

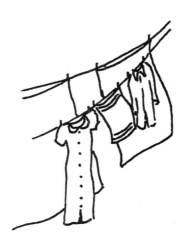

DRIFT INTO MORNING

Robin's exultation! dissolving dreaming,
  separating sleep from reluctant waker,
    singing possibilities, singing gladness —

    glory of dawning ...

Day is resurrected (for I am partner);
  night is pushed away for embrace of morning;
    these seductive moments, delicious blurrings

    cling like a lover ...

Intimations tease unreleased illusions
  caught among the shallows of lesser darkness —
    tease a drifting slumberer toward a mooring

    dealt by a robin ...

BLUXTC
(blue ecstasy)

Hunger growing through the week,
we put power into the loins
of a faded blue pickup at sunset,
BLUXTC its audacious signature,
its Chevy bed discreetly filled
with mattress, pillows, and goodies
for lesser picnics of the night.

Then sixty miles to Devil's Den,
a cave of sorts beneath two leaning,
loving rocks enormous in their mating
by swirling water, cataracts and falls
rushing through the wilderness
of Pennington Creek and a jungle
of boulders like massive bosoms
stretching toward the moon's caress
and empathy with mortal lust.

All time converged last night,
   the hours for which I was born:
   Adam to your Eve,
   Samson to a loyal Delilah,
   Caesar to your Cleopatra
   (on an Oklahoma Nile),
   Rhett Butler to a chastened Scarlett.

And we exceeded them all:
   their loves are dust;
   ours, hot and naked
   in BLUXTC bounded by moonlight
   on old and rounded, loving hills.

Our range of loving had five peaks,
   and how they shook from the roll
   of infinity in the grasp of a blueprint
   as old as urgent couplings
   in a warm and very ancient sea.

So, Teeny, where are our trophies
        for the best of loving,
        in tieing for all time?
        and though it's dawn,
        this boundary is temporary.

Morning declares my old Chevy
a carrier of night, shying when
daylight hushes giant bullfrogs
from their courtship baying,
making night air virile.
They were aphrodisiac
along the Devil's Soapdish
and set us chasing, catching,
expanding, exploding
in the Devil's Bathtub.
Lèse majesté? Likely not
(the devil has no lover)
we made it in his place.

But, Teeny, BLUXTC will mostly be
        our summer circle for the
        give and take of flexing:
        my strength serving you,
        your wonder taming me.

BIRTHDAY SIXTY-SIX

Restored by Dean last autumn: handsome fence,
   a double-posted fortress like a rock
   this January — blending redwood boards,
   some new (most old) in antiqued finishes:
   a mix of stains: the tans of youth and darks
   of age — enduring in a weary month.

The fence surrounds a garden half-asleep
   as pine and fir and juniper wear greens
   unmatched just now by bushes, lawn and beds
   in browns and dreaming of caressing warmth
   inside the acre of these friendly arms.

A little time the certain renaissance ...
   my winter burden, bleak and grey, is done —
   to lift on January thirty-one.

IN THE TIME OF CRUSADES

In spring the King and Death conspired
to send a young man off to war.

"I cannot go," the young man said,
   "my seed have not been planted."

"Nonsense," leered the king,
   "just sow your seed along the way;
   soil is waiting anywhere
      a man can take it."

"Everywhere," laughed Death.

But everywhere the soil was arid —
   hardly worth the lust for planting.
Between boredom and the battles
   he forgot (almost) the need for want

      in dust and sweat
      in catharsis of profanity
      in hack and chop.
      In success he saw
         surprise in dying.

At night unborn children
   whispered to his lonely hope,
      "survive and make us flesh."

One morning's waking was awash with joy.

   "I shall live on earth
      beyond my death," he swore.

All unconceived breathed unity
   and waited for their form
      as summer soil lay waiting
         in the fertile lap of home.

TO A LEAF

Are you grateful,
    withered leaf,
that you have a place
    to lie?

God gave you one spring
          one summer
       one fall.

You face no winter;
    are you grateful?

RETURNING TO RAPUNZEL

Rapunzel, letting down her golden hair,
   Awaits with joy his eager weight for she
Is heaven (hidden near the witch's lair)

The prince is brave, and passion fuels the dare
   When sunset challenges the youth to see
Rapunzel, letting down her golden hair.

With golden help to rise, he needs no stair
   To reach her and to find nobility
Is heaven (hidden near the witch's lair)

Her innocence and beauty spark the flare
   In finding for his ecstasy the key:
Rapunzel, letting down her golden hair.

The tower holds the rapture of the pair;
   Rapunzel longs to leave with him for he
Is heaven (hidden near the witch's lair)

When spring returns, and all the blossoms bear
   The zest of promise, this I say: to be
Rapunzel, letting down her golden hair,
Is heaven (hidden near the witch's lair)

TO A TRELLIS
(from a chauvinist vine)

I love you, polyandrous wife;
my stem roves through your diamonds,
my tendrils clasp your wooden breast,
my stamens shower you with dust.

My stem roves through your diamonds
to left or right, as with the sun;
my stamens shower you with dust —
you overlook the mess I make.

To left or right, as with the sun,
I bend by morning, afternoon.
You overlook the mess I make
when bees invade my tender parts.

I bend by morning, afternoon,
competing with two other vines.
When bees invade my tender parts,
I fantasize a hummingbird.

Competing with two other vines,
One superstrong, I find my space.
I fantasize a hummingbird
when lattice-creatures come to call.

Until October stops the curl,
my tendrils clasp your wooden breast;
supporting me has been your use;
I love you, polyandrous wife!

THE APPLE OF OUR EYE

Things will not change at our house:

    Bushes will stay where they grow,
    Trees for our lifetime are fixed,
    Pictures will stay where they hang,
    Chairs will not move — not even an inch,
    Dishes are stacked in their place,
    Comings and going are set by the clock,
    Poems, when finished, are cast in concrete.

But the mind — ah, the mind!
    And emotions are rampant not for behind;
      Together they soar while one mows,
      Together they fly while one mops.
    Private and errant, these *pas-de-deux*-sprites
Transfigure dimensions of flesh.

Up on the shingles of intentionality:
    Body, emotion and mind on the roof of our soul;
      Blending ourselves into roseate unity,
      Becoming temptation hung from a bough
    In our Garden of Eden stretched out below.
Things will not change at our house!

No ...

    Pictures will stay where they hang,
    Poems, when finished, are cast ...

MERRY VOLES AT CHRISTMAS
(a choral reading)

Narrator:
    Three dowager pussycats
    meet December 23rd.

Pussycats:
    Cat cat talk.
    Cat cat talk.

Narrator:
    Then ...

Fanci:
    So tired of mice, my dears.
    Let's CATapult tradition
    while we have a chance.
    Have you ever dined on vole?

Ali & S'ami:
    What's a vole?

Fanci:
    Something like a mouse.
    Stout, short tail, flat snout.
    I had one
    when I was just a kitten.
    It was different —
    sweeter than a mouse.
    Shall we try for vole
    on Christmas Day?

Ali & S'ami:
    Let's do it!
    Let's vole this year!

Fanci:
    But let's do it up;
    let's imagine French —
    gourmet, you know.

Narrator:
    The thought hung
    in the still December air ...

Fanci:
    My mistress did a foreign dish
    (not a vole, of course)
    and spoke the spices

as she stirred them in.
I remember some.
If I conCATenate
my distant thoughts ...

The French use lots
of melted butter ...
shallots in a body cavity ...
garnished with sherry sauce
or served with fancy mushroom gravy.
Or, simpler, we could marinate ...

Narrator: Her whiskers twitched ...
Imagination melted in her mouth.
Just who would cook those voles?
Details ... details ...

Two cats went home to wait:
one cat stayed to plot
the modus operandi for a mess
of vole December 25th.

She sought out Rump,
primo tom and mouser
of the neighborhood,
a lay-about and ne'er-do-well
except for timely talents.

Fanci: Voles are slow, I know,
and rather clumsy creatures.
But Ali, S'ami and I
are a little out of practice
for catching any kind
of fleeing Christmas dinner.
Where to catch some voles?
How to catch them?
You're so clever, Rump ...

Rump: No problem, Fanci.
I saw one at Fluffy's house

when I courted her last spring
down by the stump in the corner
where she did her caterwauling.
When I left her
(as I always leave)
I saw a vole.
Where there is one
there may be enough
for any kind of stew.
It might be fun
to pluck a few for you!

Narrator: And, Rump was responsible —
              except when taking care
              of sweet young queens
              puling for motherhood.

              So, three dowager cats
              put their faith in Rump
              to do his stuff and catch
              their Christmas dinner.

Act II

Rump: I was right; surely was.
              There IS a family of voles,
              a tasty, meaty passel
              with their silly, unmouse looks.

Narrator: But the voles began to notice.
              Rump prowled around their stump,
              nonchalant, in a phony,
              bon vivant, courting manner,
              as though he had lovin'
              on his mind.

              Awkward, cautious voles
              took counsel with each other.
              What to do?

Coal Vole: I have dark suspicions!

Soul Vole:	What does it mean?
Dole Vole:	It makes me sad to think of what could happen.
Pole Vole:	I'll stand guard and watch.
Droll Vole:	Rump is fat in winter, resting from his many romances of the year ...
Troll Vole:	Rump should get his kicked!
Voles:	Run, brothers, run; hide, sisters, hide— and stay inside. Rump is on the loose, pretending not to see us. He's in his wicked, catching mode — evil teeth and claws aflashing!
Narrator:	With danger in the Yuletide air, the voles were very careful. It was as though they could hear Fanci as she mewed a feline prayer:
Fanci:	A vole, dear Santa, and one for Ali, too. Another one for S'ami. Three will surely do for something like a Christmas stew.
Narrator:	And her co-conspirators were thinking:
Ali:	Fanci is so clever, persuading a flame of her middle years to be so gallant to her purring.

S'ami:	Fanci is so clever; she can make the nicest dishes — seasoned vole she will be stirring.
Narrator:	And, as Christmas Eve arrived, Fanci's head was full of spices she could use on those sweet voles when Rump redeemed his pledge.

Act III

Narrator:	But Rump had been sidetracked. Untimely, though it was, a new, young queen made known her need to him, and he was circling her instead of grubby voles.
Fanci:	Completely undependable! Can't depend on cats of lower class — Rump is just a tiresome ass!
S'ami:	A helpful tom is just an oxymoron!
Ali:	Now what to do?
Narrator:	There was nothing they could do. They settled for leftover mousse of mouse, which, in season's charity they shared with Rump's Christmas conquest, the homeless Persian down the street.

Pussycats:	For common food, Lord of Cats, may we be truly grateful — even when our dinner is spooned from a can.
Narrator:	The voles rejoiced, in the safety of their stump at Rump's egregious dereliction. Mice had told the voles what Fanci Cat was planning.
Voles:	*Voilà — entre nous,* no French dish of us for you! People say we're dour — there's sunshine in our hearts today. Cats were made the way they are; and, doubtless, they are here to stay.
Droll Vole:	We'll have a wary Christmas.
Narrator:	Actually, no danger lingered for the voles. Rump was complacency itself on every matter outside his macho satisfaction.
Rump:	All of us are headed to another year for cats. My heart is full for being a successful tom, and yours is filled with pussycat forgiveness.

Pussycats:	Essentially you're right, dear rounder. We'll never starve — we'll eat the best we can and not depend again on a cat with such a job description — who makes rash promises at Christmastime.
Fanci:	Let's close the year together, blending smoothness with the bumps — our hearts a truce between contriving heads and errant rumps.
Pussycats:	Cat cat talk. Cat cat talk. Meow, meow, and Merry Christmas — even to the voles!
Narrator:	And also to you ... whoever you are ...

SPRING WITHOUT END

Another spring ... small boy between
   the mystery of lying green
   in fragrant clover with a mate
   just rescued from its fallen state
   — and call to supper unforeseen.

And then ... this lad at seventeen,
   all eager smiles and sweet caffeine,
   has found another dove to fete,
   another spring ...

The mating, nesting years careen,
   but steadied by the grenadine
   of love, conspire (when time grows late)
   that memory will activate
   past warmth and fragrance to convene
   another spring ...

ON OUR WAY

Web in the head:
    cells and synapses
    sorting out
    which are cages,
    which are not.

Thought for the perfect cage:
    outpost of the mind of God
    where a raindrop
    or a snowflake
    brings down a daily
    current of unity.

Liberation days
    are playing days
    when sunshine
    bathes bars
    into invisibility
    and flesh lays
    itself on an altar
    of sweet submission.

I watch my finches
    flit and flutter
    in my/their large cage.

I watch and am watched —
    we know our places,
    and the vacuum cleaner
    takes care of overflow.

Adjacent in a smaller cage
    sits a red lory:
    saucy, judgmental,
    which bobs its head
    and raucously demands
    of its keeper,
    "What are you DOING?"

And I think,
    "I am doing what I do
    in my draped and carpeted
    container which I share
    with feathered ornaments
    making me their
    seed and grit and water."

But not for long;
    final doors are waiting
    to swing open;
    we shall escape
    and share with God
    His own splendid cage!

GENTLE FENCING

My kiss is tentative and sweet
       but meant to cheat
       your reticence
       beside a fence
with posts of lust and wires of dream.
       I see your gleam
       as more than sop
       when tied to "stop"
(because you start to be aroused)
       and I am housed
       in certainty
       of sipping thee.

RESTORATION (ON A STRING)

That time is magic which unmasks the soul.
    It strips disguises gently for a bit
        And speeds me to myself — but takes no toll.

Accretions fall away — and gone is wit;
    The drift is down into a deeper need
        Where self-inflicted mirrors show no twit

Nor troll nor monster. Surely not a weed
    Is growing toward fulfillment in the space
        Whose maker set aside for better seed.

The place of magic lies within the lace
    Of certain shadows and elusive light
        Which neither age nor wisdom will replace.

        Affirmed, the soul on string is like a kite:
        Asserting for itself the need of flight.

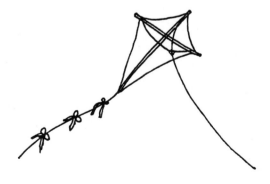

ON IT

deep tracks on carpet
flaunt disdaining snow and mud
for home and order

leaf of first clover
touches print of baby toes
carpet links new life

lawn brought to carpet
clippings with token petal
sweet work of summer

chrysanthemum falls
bronze accent precious as gold
October carpet

PRESSING THE GRASS

Stretch out and press the grass with me
for warmth invites the decorous
to taste of Spring's debauchery
in making whimsy mischievous.

When every flower fuels a buss,
stretch out and press the grass with me;
we'll let our fingers tease, and thus
begin the turn of pleasure's key.

Today is bathed in amnesty
(but waiting for an impetus);
stretch out and press the grass with me
to let our clouds turn cumulous

and moods bend yellow to discuss
the dandelions' constancy.
Buzz, bees! sing, birds! be obvious!
Stretch out and press the grass with me.

ON THE BEACH WITH THE WIDOW ZAHLER*

She found him at a lemonade stand near the boardwalk. Bronzed almost to copper, he was Teutonic: a splendid, blond, young male the likes of whom had not sired a child by her. She wasted no time in making her wish known to him. He thought her a little odd — though still a looker in middle life — and guessed her pitch a fantasy. But, what the heck, she was a lay. He agreed to meet her at the beach that night.

And, surprisingly, he did. She wasted no time with preliminaries. It was her time of the month and, with the full moon a serendipity, she was ready to get it on before he might change his mind. As it happened, he was as eager as she was ready ...

> summer loins
> tighten for flowing love
> *moon within me*

The widow Zahler felt the glow of conquest. She knew that she had been served, and served well ...

> summer body
> welcomes coded message
> *sun within me*

But from its rays will come a daughter, she thought. From this willing giant, she wanted a Brunhilda as her final child. As he hurried away, she stretched and winked at the moon. "Life is good," she said.

---

* The Widow Zahler was a fictional character who chose a different father for each of her several children. She was in a story — or, perhaps only a vignette — years ago. Author unknown.

TURQUOISE PEACE

like a painting
of the depth and breadth of God
Grand Canyon quickens visitors
to inexpressible desire for blending
with turquoise and sister silver
down from brown hands of artisans
attuned to heat, cold
               and thunder
from the Great Spirit, vastly bored
            with sophistry
              of city ways
             and selling
temporary harmony
          to those who
          tread clean slate
        in mighty deserts

THE LOQUACIOUS MOUSE

Atop an aviary stood a smaller cage
   Which housed a large white mouse
Who did more things than rodents do (except
   To mate — he had no spouse)

But Percy had a four inch friend nearby
   Who stood and glowed with joy
And seemed to listen, though she never spoke;
   She was a stylish toy.

In harem pants of rabbit fur (chapeau to match),
   This mouskin mannequin,
With yellow topaz eyes and pendant on a chain,
   Was Percy's captive djinn.

Shaheeda stood the flow of Percy's fluffy talk
   In sotto voce squeaks
Like confidences at a cocktail hour
   With trivia in peaks.

He liked to say, "A dog for a pet is almost
   As good as a mouse;
But a cat is a hissing beast, scarcely better
   Than a snake in the house!"

He liked the Clintons' politics but, with regret,
   Found Socks their cat a bitter pill;
"To strike a blow for mice in Washington,
   I could not vote for Bill!"

     Opinions dripped from Percy's lips,
      He never was a shrinker;
     Shaheeda bore them like a wife —
      She loved the little stinker!

ONE FOR FRAGRANCE

From garden to my office came
   this fruit, your name
   and scrawl: *"Surprise,*
   dear heart; how flies
the time, the season and desire
   (past summer fire);
   take these away
   but dare to say
(by leaving one for fragrance here):
   'This essence near,
   yields to arm's reach
   a yearning peach.'"

THE GRACE OF NIGHT

When sunset panders to the lure of night,
   and whispers, "Glory passes from the end
   to nibble weakness (crusting cores of might),"
   the flex of lust and flow of rest can blend.

And harvests rise by dawn, though passive gods
   admit the usury of night defies
   ambition's worm in spinning golden pods
   to make them lesser by a third their size.

Yet night prepares the palette for the brush,
   the strings to tremble for tomorrow's touch,
   erases limits in the curve of hush,
   expands the little to the grace of much.

As patterns loosed by sleep half shape our fate,
       success awakes to open morning's gate.

ON WHOSE KNEE I SIT

Beyond tomorrow matches me with song:
   discordant ego finds its proper key,
   surrenders treble glory for the strong
   demanding counterpoint awaiting me.

Goodbye, percussion's heavy tread with base
   assertive blare: the raucus self which croaks
   or moans its wanton melody to trace
   a shabby course on clefs of ribald jokes.

A rush of conscience sweeps away all sounds,
   and sharps and flats of compensation tease
   unruly notes where seeming strength abounds;
   anticipation clears the throat to please.

Though voice is thin, its halting tune when kissed
            will be the song of my ventriloquist.

FOXES OF BUCKINGHAM
(A Century-End Nursery Rhyme)

Vixen one has caught Prince Charles,
   Prince Andrew caught by vixen two;
Fox three just nipped her seven birds:
   What's the Queen to do?

      Creep, creep,
      Pounce, pounce;
      All flamingoes
      Roundly trounced;
   Frozen from their friendly pond,
   Clouds of pink come crashing down.

Diana fox has spat Charles out,
   Fergie fox has done the same;
Charles and Andrew will flit on —
   Flamingoes cannot play this game.

     Refrain

A fox has caught Prince Charles,
A fox has caught Prince Andrew,
A fox has caught the royal birds:
   Oh, what's the Queen to do?

THE THREE BEES

Johann Sebastian Bach, with mind sublime,
Could transmute anger almost anytime.
Swearing unseemly when stung in the grass,
As penance he wrote the B Minor Mass.

Beethoven reveled barefoot in a stream,
Savoring all the summer sounds as dream.
A cuckoo and a stinging bee combined —
The "Pastorale" was buzzing in his mind.

Brahms stirred the warm Vienna afternoon
With graceful, flower-tipped baton; but soon
A bee! the Kinder-Konzert went awry;
As recompense, he penned the "Lullaby."

When genius ties to place and circumstance,
A bow of splendor will result perchance;
And bees display a perfect stinger
When God Himself is in the zinger!

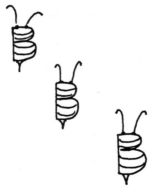

POSSIBILITIES

I tucked you sleeping, stranger,
    in the barest bedroom of my mind;
        but today (for who knows why) I wakened you
        unchanged (though I have changed)
          and placed you in a new reality.

I see you in a fresh and singing way,
    and you are with me in extension
        of the merest bygone possibility.
          Through use of you, I am making you immortal
          (to the boundaries of my own mortality).

FINGERS OF CHILDHOOD

        stilts for
     instant growth, or
   oil cans bent around shoes,
asserting self through height or clank
        of joy
                    surprise,
                 around a bale
              of prairie hay in heights
          and half-light to nest of eggs or
                    kittens
                        Rennie,
                   street of boyhood,
                  to woodland for waiting
                 mystery of thrush and dove and
                        haven
                 climbing
               catalpas with
            arms and legs embracing
       strong limbs flaunting blossom-snow of
                  summer

        power
      thunders over
   rails, snuffing out with heat
the wild and sweet verbena haunts
        of youth

DOMINION OVER THEM
(in December 1997)

Hong Kong chills and sweats despair
    with creep of potent virus.
Hysteria flowers to panic
    as bird-flu takes four lives.
A million slaughtered fowl forgotten
    haunt a cross of feathers.

GAMES

last night I closed a door;
you
did
not
know

I cat-and-moused you out
and
purred
to
sleep

there will be other nights
and
other
doors

new shell games will be played;
please
play
your
part

and if your luck holds out
as
mine
has
held

my threshold will be crossed

and
you
are
caught

GOODBYE TO A RING

A loose ring slips from my finger
      into a crowded pool of fish.
Frenzy, as flashing gold and glinting ruby
      spit from mouth to mouth.
Leave the bauble for the koi —
      old hands are past enhancement ...

THE MILLENNIUIM DOOR

The massive door is closing now.
We stretch to touch the evermore
beyond this thousand years, endow
this portal as a huge encore.

It grew from a monastic door —
the massive door is closing now.
All law and learning can ignore
the gargoyles that they disavow.

No living hands will guide a plow.
The future is no saint or whore!
The massive door is closing now
on patterns that are steeped in lore.

A brooding epitaph (in store)
sighs, "It is finished," we allow;
but have we not heard this before?
The massive door is closing now.

A LONE BOOT STRAP

These Western boots are filled with buoyant feet
tonight, possessed by spring and grace
in twirling, twist and spin
as lift and scoot
enhance
the dance.
Across one boot
in mischief's lie-low grin
are conchos on a strap in chase
around a macho foot which points a beat.
"But have you lost one strap?" someone will bleat,
"the left seems empty outer space."
Unbalance is no sin,
so in dispute
I prance,
advance
the cause acute
of swinging out and in
with single spangling I embrace:
two straps would make my world too pat, too neat.

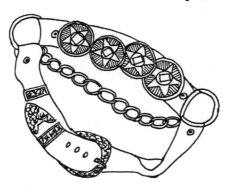

FLU IS IN THE CUCKOO'S NEST

kick the leaves

"sick — should die"
whispers the wind
"quickly — soon"
rustle yellow leaves
(the hanging few)

most have been brought low

and I am with them
on the ground
(I kick myself I guess)

NyQuil is my swill

because the willow is
switching the pyracantha
(orange berries are too
silly for so grey a day)

the ace of chills has trumped
the deuce of fever
and I am shaking
in a cloud of down

kick the leaves

just kick the leaves
but avoid the pyracantha
(thorns are guarding
every giddy berry)

walk to right or left

but kick the leaves

they
brought
down
autumn

BALLAD OF THE GREEN PRINCESS

Sam sprawled against a leaning tree,
Hardly fishing, half-awake,
Roused only by a bird, a breeze,
Or the sounds that mallards make.

Eyes were watching from the Truckee,
Googly eyes that shone with soul;
And her blood was warmed by passion
For the mortal with the pole.

Sam felt a pressure on his thigh
Like the muzzle of his dog;
Eyelids fluttered and he focused
On a green and staring frog.

Then she drew herself up proudly,
Saying sweetly as could be,
"I can be a lovely princess,
Kiss me, kiss me and you'll see."

Sam sat thunderstruck and silent
Then thrust out and caught the frog;
He laughed and said, "Of course you can,
And I'm a royal pollywog!"

"Ventrilloquist — that's it," he thought,
Peering up and down the bank;
No man (or woman) anywhere;
"I'll show the frog to Hank."

He found his fishing buddy soon,
Held the frog out in his hand;
It turned three times and looked at Sam,
Then Hank heard its sweet demand.

Hank's handsome face became a grin;
"Kiss it! Kiss it! — man, you dog!"
"Naw," said Sam, "I figure at my age
She's worth more to me a talking frog."

Unkissed, a hapless Hildegard,
    Sitting on a velvet pad,
    Became the darling of TV —
    Sam, the richest kind of cad.

She was brilliant, she was witty
    And her voice was like a song;
    She was mother, lover, angel —
    Perfect wisdom made her strong.

She was reticent about herself
    Except to tell her name;
    She seemed to be from far away
    And loved the challenge of the game.

But Sam grew tired and took her home
    To keep her as his own;
    Curiosity destroyed greed,
    He was ready to atone.

Though strong contrition filled his heart,
    Elder pride led him astray;
    To bring himself to give the kiss —
    "There must be some other way ...

Hildegard," he said, "please tell me
    Who you are and why you're here."
    She caught a mosquito while she thought
    And then she said, "My dear,

That sunny day you won my heart,
    Smiling as you held the pole —
    No longer young and yet your face
    Was a window to your soul.

I was Hildegard of Bingen,
    Born nine hundred years ago;
    I was abbess of a convent —
    No princess — now you know.

Ecstatic visions ruled my life
    Until the very end;

I had one just before I died:
Light from a celestial friend.

I was told I could continue
In the body you see here,
Sharing visions — doing good,
With no danger, with no fear.

For God rules behind a pattern
Of exceptions to His law;
His strength is in 'the least of these' —
A frog is not a flaw.

And I am a lovely woman
When I am out of green;
I pretend I am a princess
Because it makes a man so keen.

Come, Sam, and let me touch your face."
What was Sam to do? He did!
His years from thirty rolled away!
(Who would want to be a kid?)

He bent down again and kissed her
And a veil was torn away;
He saw her through the eyes of God —
Creative aura still at play.

The shimmer of a smile divine
Entered softly into him
For he knew her very essence
In head and heart and limb.

"From now," said Hildegard, "you've
Forty years to savor
The vision of a perfect woman —
May it give them flavor.

So, Sam, addio and goodbye;
With good begun, I go;
Think of me as I of you —
My next river is the Po!"

SPRING FROLIC

Slinging bags of steer manure
　　for the greening of the yard
　　for a bigger, yellow daffodil
　　for a sweeter, redder rose!

Aeration of the ground
　　thatching of the turf
　　turning of the soil for bedding
　　for the seeds and bulbs and hope.

For the work of spring is sowing
　　for the summer joy of crowing
　　high upon our fence of duty
　　when our victory is beauty.

So, we're

　　slinging bags of steer manure
　　for the greening of the yard
　　for a bigger, yellow daffodil
　　for a sweeter, redder rose!

FLIGHT OF EGO

He

is lost

who never

cast a shadow

or never saw time

stand still in his image,

proving, with a looking glass,

substance among insubstantial

gossamers, transparencies and wraiths

of companions bogged in blurred existence.

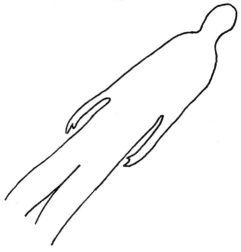

DIRGE FOR A FLY

Alas,
your juices sucked
by a rough marauding
spider clutching an ex-maggot —
tough shit

NAOMI DUNCAN

My people were called hewers of wood
and carriers of water,
but my young prospector Olaf
looked at me through softer eyes.

When the forces of Major Savage
drove Ahwahneeches from Yosemite
to the reservation in 1851
I hid and stayed and watched and waited.

Into this lovely valley Olaf came
as the full moon of early summer
flooded our majestic Eden.
My Swedish Adam's hair was like a halo
as he lifted me on beams of earthly light
arising from his deepest being,
and I became his radiance.

So it was for a season.
In yellow October,
from the valley for supplies,
Olaf was cut down by my brother.

I married Olaf's best friend Thomas
who sheltered me from tribal shame.
We raised three strong sons
and one fair daughter
for the new state of California.

Visitor to Yosemite,
the bones of an Indian woman lie below.
In a graceful moment, my good husband
caught in stone
the purest fire of all my life,
    HAPPY THE WOMAN WHO HAS
        BEEN TO HEAVEN TWICE

Friend, two men were necessary.

FRISKY BUCK

A bunnymaker all the way
(For age will scarcely slow his hop)
He finds sweet does for interplay
And fills their feisty need nonstop.

This rover has quick charm to swap:
A bunnymaker all the way
At hidden glen or mountaintop,
By darkest night or brightest day.

He kicks his heels and winks, "Olé!"
Delight in conquest seems to prop
A bunnymaker all the way
Through years of playing frequent pop.

He plants his seed which yields a crop
For diners catching their entrée.
His virtue: pleasure as a sop —
A bunnymaker all the way!

FROM WALLS OF MEMORY

Tapping on a distant wall
    (desolation muffled but insistent)

Is it Fidelio? or Mary, Queen of Scots?
    perhaps the prisoner of Chillon?
        or the man in the iron mask?

It is communion of the hopeless,
    a fantasy in sound
which only God decodes
    (but seems unmoved)

    I despair with each.

But ... likely none of the above;
    we have no political prisoners
        in the library except
        those pressed into print.

The tapping, stopped, resumes;
    orientation gains control
      — the nearby gallery
    is communicating.

Its message is coming into focus
    — works of art are being hung
        for a new exhibit.

These are lesser pictures ...

ACCOMMODATION

They pretend to
Enjoy the pastimes of their mates —
They pretend to.

But leaps through hoops of duty do
Not make success of tiresome dates
Though they suppress their tepid hates —

They pretend to.

FAMILY CIRCLE

A shirtless boy of twelve, hip-deep in wheat,
Is gazing into manhood from a field,
Assurance shaping smiling lips as heat
Of August promises a double yield.

In T-shirt, jeans and jaunty slouch, he grins
At thirty, sure and safe in openness,
His manhood proved without excessive sins,
His arms are strong when reaching for success.

Much like a justice sitting straight and tall
With warm patrician smile, he strokes the years;
"Though forty-nine is late, let's throw the ball —
We'll fetch it, Rover, 'til it disappears!"

And so, three desk-top photographs can say
Three blessings to an older self than they.

ON CATCHING 22

I'm the best darn mouser
in these parts;
I don't eat 'em,
I just delete 'em.
First I cheese 'em,
then I squeeze 'em,
just call me Trapper Zap!

WHATEVER HAPPENED TO VERNON HOWELL?

The piper of the "seven seals" is dead,
The mesmerizing psychopath who fed
   His sheep on insecurity with hope,
A Judas goat to all who would be led.

Betrayal spread on Waco winds to sell
Apocalypse when David Koresh fell;
   As terror-stricken children burned alive,
A gentle bullet kissed his soul to Hell.

So ends a Texas dropout playing God,
Who sowed and reaped in thin, receptive sod,
   Who watered with his messianic greed —
Whose final harvest was an empty pod.

AUTUMN LIFT

I am drying up from length of summer
    but resist October's coming
                  for rains reflect
    new wine in an old bottle

this willful juice emboldens
                with the flaming of the days
    when colors' gaudy-whispers
            translate "now" into "forever"

a little wrestling in the leaves
            a modest imprint briefly —
blown away on a windy night
           into another dimension

CONSCIENCE OF A LOVER

"It is the fault of time," I cried, "that fate
Has brought you to me forty years beyond
Those lusty nights of youth; alas, this late
Temptation bows beyond my need to bond."

    "Unfair," I sighed, "unleashing lust on one
    Whose tender years invite the thrust of time
    To make the ring replete when all is done.
    This is not love — just empty pantomime."

        "But if the message come, 'Yet stay awhile,'
        My sail shall rise and give itself to winds
        Whose force is fed by innocence and guile
        To hurry us where newer time begins."

So passion shall be shaped with reason's glove,
And logic strengthened by a touch of love.

AND THIS IS HEAVEN

My soul is joined precisely to its place
In superconductivity unknown
On earth, reserved in God's magnetic lace
Which reaps each mortal speck which He has sown.

How can my speck contain it:
surging of celestial power,
vastness of God Himself as I extend by one
the circuit holding all who ever lived?

All mysteries are solved, all knowledge known,
Subsumed in rush of disembodied joy
When current from the mind of God has proved
My soul is joined precisely to its place.

EAGLES & ROSES

Athena is curled in my chair;
  I touch her cheek and she smiles
    as she says, "Bring me a rose."

I say, "But it's winter, my dear,"
  and she says, "For lovers, there is no winter —
    only two eagles soaring below summer clouds,
      lifting on light winds of love
        as our hearts lift like the flames on this hearth.
        Bring me a rose!"

Her will is mine, and I move to the piano.
  A song begins as my fingers find petals,
    and the room fills with her rose.
      Her laughter blends with the notes:
        "'Tis the last rose of summer"
        and our voices rise together.

My reward is the promise of spring.
                      Behold my wings!

1926-

These years were mine for I am blest
to blend my voice with "Auld Lang Syne"
this year 2000 and attest
    these years were mine.

A twig became a questing vine
through Oklahoma fences — zest
for nature, school and lonely wine.

All came together in a crest
of mind and flesh to intertwine;
and reaching out has manifest
    these years were mine.

ALL THE WORLD'S A CAGE

A cage you say? Oh, surely not!
My wings can log ten thousand miles,
Speeding to the Land of Polyglot
To nestle in a curve of smiles
On lips which say, "There is no cage."

What thinking man would fashion wire
And steadfast perches for his place?
Do cups of certainty inspire
A song above a papered space?
He sings? He also builds a rage!

And yet I touch a paradox:
Though from each cage there is a view,
The cheer within false freedom mocks
The singing of its ingenue
(For she is captive of one role)

And I am trapped in mine to play
A scrap of time in flesh and guess —
Shortchanged, accepting a bouquet
Of space disguising emptiness —
While clinging to a tepid soul.

Glory to the vision that can make
Small cages intimate and kind,
Can see the uttermost opaque
But, friend of moments, be unblind
To kinship with a finch or dove.

When feathered bosoms burst with joy
On twig or perch, the mating rite
Ordained is neither caged nor coy;
Then you become my wings for flight
And I, container for your love.

LAMENTS TO PRESIDENTS

Carter's Lance and Reagan's Meese,
Sleek and plump and gracious geese,
Proclaim deserving loyalty
From White House webfoot royalty.

FINAL BLOOM

Some, willing, move to self-Gethsemane
    At midnight bed or blazing matinee
But dread the blooming of their gallows tree.

Dark garden of despair, is there a key
    To lock of gloom? a reason to unsway
Some willing move to self-Gethsemane?

Estranged and banished grope for clemency
    Where even greys and failures interplay
But dread the blooming of their gallows tree.

Forget the sunlight and calliope;
    From rich, the weary turn in disarray;
Some, willing, move to self-Gethsemane.

Forget the lost who love facsimile,
    Who hold a competence that skews astray
But dread the blooming of their gallows tree.

The bigger garden calls the absentee:
    The witless, feckless, foolish who obey
Some willing move to self-Gethsemane
But dread the blooming of their gallows tree.

DOUBLE DUDGEON AT A RAFFLE

A

PILL   WON

THE

LOVE   CHAIN

QUIL

AFRICAN GREY CHRISTMAS

There on Christmas morning
　　Beside the glowing tree:
A gift without a tag —
　　Its source a mystery.

The cage stood black and tall,
　　A parrot sat within
And stared at all who stared,
　　Its feathers grey as tin.

It had one bit of flash:
　　A tail of Christmas red;
Its eyes were light as straw:
　　Gems in a heavy head.

It blinked and spread its beak —
　　Thick dark tongue a-flicking;
Every ear was waiting,
　　The only sound was ticking.

Like a prima donna
　　As she prepares to sing,
The bird adjusted slightly
　　And archly shook each wing.

It wagged its big head wisely,
　　Bending without delay —
And then it rent the silence:
　　LEAN YOUR EAR THIS WAY

DON'T YOU TELL A SINGLE SOUL
HO, HO, HO
GOOD WILL TO MEN
MAY NOTHING YOU DISMAY
ALL IS CALM
HO, HO, HO
'TIS THE SEASON
HARPS OF GOLD
AND PEACE TO MEN ON EARTH
DASHING THROUGH THE SNOW
ALL IS BRIGHT
HO, HO, HO

Everyone clapped and laughed
And wished it Christmas cheer;
And thus to you, my friend,
And have a ho, ho year!

THE MASTER CALLER
After Kipling's "L'Envoi"

When earth's last caller has finished
    And the final tip has been done,
When the strains of music have faded
    And the lights have dimmed on the fun,
We shall rest; and how we shall need it —
    Lie down for an aeon or two,
Till the Master of All Good Dancers
    Shall bid us to dance anew!

And those who are called shall be happy
    (They are light and endless and free)
They shall twirl in a world beyond evening
    Which only dancers can see;
Their caller shall be only the Greatest —
    In space beyond dance-floor and hall;
They shall dance for an age without stopping
    And never be tired at all!

And only the Master shall praise us,
    And only the Master shall blame,
And no one shall dance for duty,
    And no one shall dance for fame;
But each for the joy of movement
    And each in his separate star,
Shall do the dance as he feels it
    For the God of Things as They Are!

NOTES

NOTES

NOTES

NOTES

NOTES